CONSUMER
ORGANIZATION OF
DISABLED PEOPLE OF NFLD. & LAB.

rawnie dunn

Funny You Should Ask
Living with a disability

Copyright: Council of Canadians with Disabilities, 1996

Cover art and design: Marc Baur

Publication Data:
Dunn, Rawnie, 1956

Title:
Funny You Should Ask - Living with a disability

ISBN 0-9680869-0-X

Published by:
The Consumer Organization of Disabled People of
Newfoundland and Labrador
St. John's, NF, 1996

Dedication

To the Disabled Consumer Movement in Canada

Contents

FOREWORD

When I first met Rawnie Dunn, she and I had the usual chat about what we did. "I'm a writer," she said. That did not come as a complete surprise, as I had enjoyed reading her stories in *Transition*, a newsletter of the BC Coalition of People with Disabilities (BCCPD) for several years. What did surprise me was finding out about the circumstances in which she pursued this daunting career.

Most writers have a space, if not a room, if not a Gulf Island, to themselves; somewhere they can hole up for hours or days at a time and allow the Muse to work her many wonders. Rawnie had, as I recall, part of the top of a desk immediately adjacent to the kitchen in her apartment. And no ordinary kitchen, either, but one frequently occupied by two boys and a dog engaged in repeated primordial struggles for sustenance. Rawnie, of course, provided the sustenance and arbitrated the struggles, and did a fair measure of household and family maintenance following both. I remember wheezing for breath as a result of merely spectating at a few of the more typical episodes.

The idea of trying to write in the midst of this swirl of activity did—and does—fill me with awe. Still, one mustn't be too critical; those two boys have been willing to down weapons long enough to be the first and most demanding audience for each of her stories over the years, and thereby deserve some credit for what appears here.

And then there's this thing about disability.

I have told my friend on more than one occasion that she is the most disabled person I've ever known. She always accepts this comment as a compliment. There is on first approach the wheelchair. But Rawnie has surprises waiting: a hearing impairment that would make her immune to the unexpected appearance of Twisted Sister performing live in her living room, and waves of fatigue that can knock her out in mid-sentence and reduce the non-kitchen time of the day to a few precious moments. You will read in these stories personal experiences of all these disabilities, and more.

Perhaps it is that breadth of experience that has given Rawnie the source of insight that shines through these stories, and indeed her work over many years as a disabled activist: an abiding interest in the everyday reality of disability, the ways in which persons with disabilities configure and take control of their lives, and in the social processes which create and reinforce handicaps. These are the issues which she conveys through this collection of writing.

As a writer and an advocate, Rawnie has played a role in the movement in Canada of persons with disabilities defining themselves and their goals. She has, as you will see, attended meetings and spoken for the rights of disabled persons wherever an agenda, a microphone, and—oh, yes a hotel room with an accessible washroom—beckoned. And, throughout, she has kept writing. The days of exclusion from society, from education and employment, the days of the charity telethons, started to end when persons with disabilities, like Rawnie, began to speak out.

And those days may end, when, like Rawnie, we find in them sources of laughter. For if there is content in these stories, there is also style. The style of a humorist. You will find in these stories an observant eye, but an eye with a gleam in it. That is a great gift. So great, in fact, that it seems it can get you through quite a few bouts of Kitchen Wars.

Peter Carver
Vancouver, 1996

WITH FRIENDS LIKE THESE . . .

Designing Disasters

Enthusiasm is a wonderful thing. When it's in a talented and caring person, it's unstoppable. My mother is a case in point. She's been a fashion designer for years and she's come up with many beautiful, original designs. She also cares about the problems people with disabilities can face getting into and out of clothing and has set herself the task of helping to solve some of those problems.

All of this is certainly praiseworthy and I don't wish to complain, but it's just that she always wants a disabled person to test her creations. And it's always me. For example, when she designed a pair of pants with a system of hooks and pulleys so the wearer wouldn't have to bend over to pull them up, I'm the one who had to go out in them. The system worked fine, but I looked like a building under construction. Another time she created a top with a neckline so loose that it would flop over the head and settle into a position without any tugging or straining. The trouble was that after it flopped over my head it kept on going until it settled into a position around my knees. She has also created many designs of clothing that will come off easily. Very easily. Like if you breath. Often, I have gone out with more snaps in my clothing than there are in an exotic dancer's.

A week before my last birthday, she presented me with a pair of jeans she'd made with the problems some people with disabilities have in public restrooms, in mind. Everything was designed for speed in undressing. The underwear was fastened with Velcro to the inside of the jeans and a 24 inch zipper ran across the back and down one leg. The idea was: one quick unzip and presto, the entire back falls away like the flap on a baby's sleepers! I wore them when I went to a special lecture on my birthday. Just before the lecture was to start, I nipped into the washroom to test my jeans again. They worked perfectly and I was very happy with them until it came time to zip them back up again and the zipper stuck. Someone must have wondered why I stayed in the wash-room for the entire lecture. I'd probably be there still if a good friend hadn't happened by. I will be eternally grateful to her (but I do wish she hadn't laughed quite so loudly).

As commendable as her intentions are, I wasn't too sad when, after learning about the birthday incident, my mother swore to stop designing special clothing. That was only a few months ago, but yesterday she called to tell me about her newest invention for people with disabilities.

"I've got this marvelous idea," she said excitedly, "for crutches. You know how you always say that you move too jerkily to use crutches? Well, these ones don't have to be lifted off the ground and repositioned every time you take a step. You see, they have little wheels on the bottom. I want you to test them for me."

I can hardly wait.

The Miracle Drug

Naomi has been one of my closest friends for years. She's always there ready and willing to lend a helping hand, give me a pat on the shoulder, or, if need be, provide one of her own to cry on. Whenever I feel like a good chat or watching a movie with someone, she's my first choice. Yet, sometimes, I have to resist the temptation to pull down the shades and hide in the bathroom when I see her approaching.

Naomi, you see, is a health faddist. Every health-related craze that's come along in the years I have known her—like copper bracelets, Rolfing, hair-analysis, iris-reading, and Primal Screaming, to name but a few—she has religiously adopted while demanding that I convert too. It's not really

5

the craze that bothers me—a few of them may actually have some merit—it's just that she gets so, well, crazy about it.

For example, her latest craze has been for "mineral therapies". Anything from a chronic disabling condition to a predisposition to dislike the rain, Naomi would attempt to cure with a mineral pill.

"The 'to-do' in Palestine," she recently asserted, "is caused by a diet deficient in tungsten, you know."

For the sake of world peace, I offered to send them my toaster; but she was not amused. When she says a thing like that the only thing I can do is try to ignore it, but sometimes it's a strain.

Last month, my whole family came down with the three-week-flu and Naomi sprang to the rescue. Every night she came over with a new batch of mineral bottles which she crammed into the bathroom. We had magnesium, manganese, dolomite, iodine, and anything else that could be chipped out of the ground, in there. Whenever I opened the medicine cabinet I felt like I should be wearing a helmet with a light on it. Finally, I told her that I couldn't take anything because I was adhering to a very strict regimen myself. THAT, she could respect, so she asked me about it.

"It's wonderful!" I said. "If I feel depressed, bored, fatigued, over-worked, or under-appreciated, I pop one of these things into my mouth and feel instantly better!"

She was interested.

"You do have to control the dosage." I continued, "It's potent stuff—but its effect is nothing short of miraculous.

Why, just yesterday I used it to curb an oncoming fit of hysteria!"

"And it worked?" Naomi asked, wide-eyed.

"Absolutely!" I avowed. "Proper use of it could prevent a war—in my home, anyway."

"Whoa!" she cried, impressed. "What is it?"

"It's called `chocolate'," I said and watched her pale.

It was an unkind thing to do. I felt sorry as she wordlessly piled all her mineral bottles into a plastic garbage bag and left with it. I will definitely apologize to her the next time I see her, which should be in about three weeks. Right now, she's got the flu.

A Touch Of Magic

or: How I Came to Stop Hating Baseball

People coming to my house look a little confused. At first glance, my home seems to be the abode of a romantic recluse. Messily stuffed bookcases have been crammed into every crevice. Little replicas of thatched cottages perch on book shelves, the tops of cupboards, and the walls. Flouncy fabrics and brass candlesticks are strewn throughout. However, scattered amongst the doilies and the fake antiques is an assortment of baseball paraphenalia. My friends' eyebrows always rise when they see this salute to Jock-land. They may think they understand the bats cluttering the hallway, the catcher's mitt on the stove, and the baseball magazines on the bathroom floor when they remember that I have two young sons, but they are always very surprised when they encounter the framed 8 x 10 of the "Los Angeles' Dodgers" on my desk.

Yes, the picture is mine—so are the magazines—but I can explain. You see, it all started not so long ago. In the spring of '88, a baseball-fanatic friend, who had been trying for years to interest me in The Game without much success, decided to "play dirty". Without my knowledge, he enrolled my 11 year old in the local Little League. The boy was ecstatic. Bats and balls and evening practices quickly became his life. My life, just as quickly, became one of laundering uniforms at night and shivering through twilight games.

I even started watching some of the professional games on TV with the guys. I figured that if I sprinkled in a "great play!" now and then no one would know that I never so much as focused my eyes on the action. That illusion was shattered one day when, after reading `AL WEST' on the stadium wall, I turned to my companions and asked innocently: "just who is this `Al West' anyway?" The flurry of male laughter that was unleashed was utterly humiliating.

From then on, I studied every baseball article and story I came upon. By late September, I knew the names of all the main Major League players, where and for whom they played, and the standings of all the teams in both the Eastern and Western Divisions of the American League (AL EAST & AL WEST) and the National League. Unfortunately, I'd still not developed any affection for what I called under my breath "the most useless waster-of-time imaginable." True, once when my son made a spectacular game-winning outfield catch, I was so excited that I nearly threw myself out of my wheelchair. But then, I'd reacted the same way when my

9

other son came home from school and announced that his class had won a pizza lunch.

Nevertheless, when I was invited to a World Series TV party I saw the chance to redeem myself. The Oakland Athletics were playing against the Los Angeles' Dodgers so I diligently studied the players, the managers, and the historical background of these teams. This time, I was going to impress everyone with my baseball knowledge.

A few hours before the first Series games it occurred to me that it would probably be more effective if I seemed to care one way or the other about who won. So I tried to decide which team to root for. I was going through the obvious factors—which team had the nicer uniform, which team had the more attractive players, etc.—when I remembered something I'd read about baseball teams once. The article had disparaged teams that sometimes relied willy nilly on a touch of magic—"like the Dodgers"—and ended with the wish that Baseball itself would come "into the 20th Century."

This is the complaint about so many things today. Although, in the past, the recipe for success had always been 10% inspiration to 89% perspiration with a dash of good luck thrown in as a spice, nowadays it seems that everything that can't be entered into some well-ordered data column gets tossed onto the mumbo-jumbo heap.

Suddenly, Baseball made sense to me! That is, 'Baseball', I realized, wasn't SUPPOSED to make complete sense! Its essence was unpredictability! Being a willy nilly sort myself, I decided to root for the Dodgers. The team that believed in a touch of magic.

Towards the end of that first game it was not looking too good for my chosen team, though. They were behind by one run and it seemed like they might lose not only this first game but the whole Series as well. To make matters worse, the Dodgers' star batter, Kirk Gibson, had been forced to sit out the entire game with a multitude of "disabling" injuries. The Dodgers were at bat in the bottom of the ninth—final— inning. Although they had a runner on the bases near the end of the game, it did not look like another batter would bring him home. When there were two out, everybody thought it would very soon be all over.

Then the Dodgers' manager, Tom Lasorda, did one of the most startling things I've ever seen. He took the next batter out and replaced him with a player who had never even left the dugout yet: Kirk Gibson.

Now, I'm not much older than Mr. Gibson, but he reminds me of my son. They both have hair that stands up in cowlicks when they exercise and there is the same look of perpetually cheerful confusion about them. Also, my son, who plays left field like Gibson does, idolizes him. So it was with a kind of maternal apprehension that I watched Kirk Gibson hobble out to the plate on his injured legs. The crowd started cheering wildly and Gibson looked abashed but hopeful.

"STRIKE ONE" was called but the crowd continued to cheer. I silently cursed the crowd for setting Gibson up for a major—maybe even traumatic—disappointment. When "STRIKE TWO" was called, I mentally chastised Lasorda for allowing this to happen to the poor guy. `A little faith in magic,' I angrily told Lasorda, `may be a good thing but it wouldn't hurt for you to get a little real too, you know!' A few foul balls simply prolonged the agony.

11

Then on the last strike of the final inning of the game, Gibson hit the ball—hard. It looked like a small white satellite as it floated over the barrier and into the crowd of fans. It made a home run for Gibson. It also brought the other runner home, and the game to a dramatic, fairytale end.

The Dodgers had won by a single run. People were screaming, caps were being hurled into the air, and the other Dodgers had leapt to their feet and were streaming onto the field to surround Gibson. What impressed me most, though, was the look on Gibson's face as he trotted around the bases. That look was the most wonderful mixture of joy, triumph, and incredulity. It was that look which turned me into a devoted baseball fan in one night and it is a picture of that look which graces my desk. It is a constant reminder to me of the power of an unpredictable, willy nilly faith in a touch of magic.

THE 'T' WORD

Transportation: Troubles and Triumphs

The Ten "Do's" Of Airline Travel For Passengers With Disabilities

N UMBER ONE "DO"

I have to start this off with a confession: there are only nine "Do's" in here. However, articles of this type are always about the "ten" of something—never the "nine". "Nine" is not the kind of number you can use at the heading of an article like this. It looks incomplete; it makes people nervous. If I had called this THE NINE "DO'S" OF AIRLINE

TRAVEL you would wonder: 'What happened to the tenth one? Did she lose it? Is there a disembodied "Do" somewhere out there? Or maybe,' you would worry, as a twitch crept into your cheek muscles, 'it was censored?' Then you would add it to your list of things to agonize over when you lie in bed at night wishing you could fall asleep. So, in the interest of your peace-of-mind, I pretended there are ten of these things, although you now know there are really only nine. So, I guess we should be moving along now to NUMBER TWO "DO".

NUMBER TWO "DO"

When planning your trip, DO UNDER-PACK. Your goal is to take only one bag or knapsack that you carry with you at all times. This is because, whether you are in an airport or a hotel, the second you put your bag down someone will snatch it up, carry it 5 feet, drop it again, and hold out their palm for a tip. Also, at the end of every flight, there is an announcement demanding that "passengers requiring assistance" remain seated long enough to allow the other passengers to deplane and negotiate refugee status, and Flight Attendants to bid each other emotional farewells. Meanwhile, your luggage is all by itself going around and around in a place which is frequented by luggage-thieves. So, it is important to take only what you can carry. This takes some practice but you can do it. I did. After several years of travel, I learned to leave things like matching shoes, underwear, hearing aid batteries, I.D., and return tickets at home.

NUMBER THREE "DO"

When on an airplane, DO SAY "YES" to everything the Flight Attendant offers you. As a hearing impaired person who can never seem to understand what waiters in restaurants are asking me, I'd found it was a good idea to say 'no, thank you' to any offered extras. In this way, I avoided getting the Blowtorch-Hot Special Sauce on my sandwich and lemon squeezed into my milky tea. Airlines, however, are different. They do not offer extras—not in the Economy section, anyhow—they offer basics. So, say "yes" to those pillows the Flight Attendants offer before takeoff, say "yes" when they offer you something to eat with, and say "yes" when they offer to land the plane before you disembark.

NUMBER FOUR "DO"

DO CULTIVATE "FAMILIES" among the personnel at those airports you visit a lot. It's easy to do this. First, choose the person you want to be your aunt/uncle/in-law, etc., and ask their name, the names and birthdays of their spouse and children, and other anniversaries. Record this information and remember to send cards on those days. Whenever you arrive at their airport bring them inflated balloons and fudge. Having "family" at several airports will help you to relieve the boredom of stopovers, get personal attention, and make airports more homey. Be prepared for a little tragedy, though. The people which I chose as my "family" members must all have been born under the same unlucky star because every time I show up they mutter, "Domestic emergency—gotta go," and take off in the other direction.

NUMBER FIVE "DO"

If you use a wheelchair, DO RESTRICT YOUR USE OF THOSE WHEELCHAIRS USED TO TAKE YOU TO YOUR SEAT ON THE PLANE. In fact, you should refuse to be in one more than a maximum of ten feet away from the airplane. It's not that they are about as comfortable as park benches; neither is it that they look like the product of the mating of a barstool and the national flag. No, it's for a far deadlier reason. It may seem harmless enough to stay in it and let a stranger whizz you about the airport. However, let me illustrate with a personal example what can happen to you if you do this: Once I arrived in Ottawa after an all-day flight. Like many passengers who use wheelchairs, I spent the last hours of the flight counting the minutes until I got to an accessible airport washroom. When we finally landed, I figured I could save a few seconds by asking an airport attendant to wheel me directly to a washroom without transferring me to my own chair first. To my cries of "Faster! Faster!", she raced through the airport until she deposited me in the centre of a spacious accessible washroom. Then she said she'd return in ten minutes and left while locking the door as she closed it. It was only then that I realized that airplane wheelchairs do not have large side wheels and cannot be self-propelled.

NUMBER SIX "DO"

There is an old Star Trek episode in which the crew members get a strange disease which brings the most repressed parts of their personalities to the surface. Once affected, the hyper-logical Spock starts blubbering about his childhood and gentle Sulu becomes a Samurai warrior. This disease really exists. It is known as "Confinedus Airspaceus" and attacks passengers on long airplane flights. After a few hours of coping with shimmying floors, artificial breezes, and people with plasticized smiles, airline passengers can lose touch with reality and have a hidden part of their personality take over. I have encountered many cases of Confinedus Airspaceus in my travels. For example, I have met a rock musician who began the flight as a C.E.O., and a used car salesman turned politician. (Outside of B.C., I understand, this is not the norm.) I even met a somber Secretary of State employee who became a Robin Williams clone and draped a paper with ZZZZZZZ written on it over my face as I slept.

There are two things you should do about this disease:

1. In order to stop people from blubbering all over you, DO WEAR YOUR HEADPHONES. Whether or not you actually listen to anything is irrelevant. Headphones are the most potent stop signal our society has. Even the most severely infected person will respect them and leave you alone.

2. Secondly, before your flight, DO HEAVILY SEDATE YOURSELF. You are vulnerable to this disease too, you know, and may behave in a way that you will spend the rest of your days trying to live down.

NUMBER SEVEN "DO"

The best "DO" for avoiding painful trips is one that should be practised long before your flight is booked. Whenever you are at any meeting and they ask for a volunteer to go somewhere unusual DO PRETEND YOU HAVE JUST TURNED TO STONE. Do not respond even if they beat you. Eventually, like the Canadian grizzly, they will tire of pestering an inanimate object and find another victim. If fossilization is not your style, there are other ways of achieving the same result. Some people prefer to grab their throat and dash to the washroom while making "kecking" sounds; others have successfully isolated themselves by bursting into loud and embarrassing sobs. Just make sure you do not end up as The Volunteer. I never could practice what I preach, though. As soon as anyone asks for a volunteer, I begin bouncing up and down in my chair with one arm thrashing in the air above my head and the other pointing at myself. Because of this, I have:

- slept all night on the dining hall stage of a B.C. camp and woke up to find myself being observed by a hundred diners as they ate breakfast;

- been at the mercy of the Room Service of a hotel in Saskatoon that was straight out of *Whatever Happened to Baby Jane?* and which did things like garnish my pancakes with a large dead spider;

- spent two weeks as the only wheelchair-user in a monastery in Quebec where the only toilet cubicle large enough to accommodate a wheelchair was in the monks' private washroom.

NUMBER EIGHT "DO"

At the beginning of this article I said there were nine "Do's". That wasn't entirely true. Due to circumstances beyond my control—such as lack-of-imagination—I am going to have to omit one more "Do". I hope you don't think I would deliberately deceive you, though. Believe me, this hurts me more than it does you but I'm afraid you have to forget about NUMBER EIGHT and go on to the next one.

NUMBER NINE "DO"

Um, er, there's nothing here either. Uh, you see, cough-cough, I've had a really rough day and, well, um, maybe I lied, just a little.

NUMBER TEN "DO"

Ok, ok. A lot.

Pssst, Can You Keep A Secret?

(PLEASE NOTE: IF YOU ARE EMPLOYED BY THE AIR-LINES, DO NOT READ THIS. It will be very boring and irrelevant to you. You have much more valuable things to do with your time like reading travel brochures or dreaming about someday being able to park your own 747 beside the Volkswagen in your garage. This is only for airline passengers who use wheelchairs. So, you others, SHOO!).

. . . **N**ow that they have gone, I will tell you a secret. This is something I learned while doing the Conference Hop for national organizations like the Council of Canadians

21

with Disabilities (CCD), the National Educational Association of Disabled Students (NEADS), and the DisAbled Women's Network of Canada (DAWN-Canada). Lean a little closer and I will whisper it to you: The airline personnel that board passengers onto the airplane but do not fly HATE having to transfer wheelchair-users onto those skinny little chairs with casters on the bottom and taking them down the aircraft aisle to their seats. They will be perfectly friendly and helpful on the surface but if you pay attention you will notice that they can never seem to find the chair when they need it, and feel much too busy to bother with all that rigamarole anyway.

NO, NO, DON'T LEAN BACK AGAIN MUTTERING 'SO WHAT?' THIS is the fundamental premise to a game which, when played right, will land wheelchair-using passengers who pay Economy Fares into the Executive or Business Class section.

AHH, I see I've got your attention again. So, here's what you need to play:

- an Economy ticket
- a fancy outfit
- your own wheelchair

Here's how you play: When you check in, the clerk will ask you to transfer to an airline wheelchair right then and there. POLITELY BUT FIRMLY REFUSE TO DO SO. After you go down to the boarding gate, scrutinize the personnel at the counter and make a bee-line for the most tired-looking one. Attach yourself to that person. Draw attention to the fact that she or he is tired with friendly remarks like: "BOY, IS IT BUSY IN HERE! I BET YOU'RE BEAT!" or "GEE, IT SURE IS A SHAME THAT YOU HAVE TO SLAVE AWAY IN HERE ON SUCH A FINE DAY!" etc.

When your Target asks if you need to be transferred to an airline wheelchair to get to your seat, sigh and say: "YES, I'M AFRAID SO. MY WHEELCHAIR WILL ONLY GO UP TO THE FIRST AISLE." (This is true for almost all wheelchairs.)

Now the game begins in earnest. Your Target will quickly assess you, his or her co-workers, and whether or not there is an unbooked seat somewhere in the Upper Class section. If these checks indicate that the chances of pulling it off are good, SHE OR HE WILL TAKE YOU TO THE FIRST ROW AISLE SEAT (not the unbooked seat), HELP YOU TRANSFER INTO IT, WHISK AWAY YOUR WHEELCHAIR, AND HURRIEDLY LEAVE.

In a little while, the man or woman (almost always a man) whose seat you now occupy will come in. This is why you have dressed up. You want him to think that you have another seat in the Snazzy Class section and were accidently put in the wrong place. You definitely do not want him to bellow, "HEY, WHAT'S THE BUM DOING IN MY SEAT?"

When he confronts you, smile and say, "Oh, I'm TERRIBLY sorry! I must have the wrong seat! I'll get out of it just as soon as I can get my wheelchair back and a couple of Flight Attendants who have the time to..."

DON'T ACTUALLY CALL ANY FLIGHT ATTENDANT, THOUGH. It won't be necessary. By this time, Mr. Executive will be feeling pretty childish about making such a fuss about his seat and will be quite willing to retire to the unbooked seat voluntarily.

Then, relax in a big seat, eat fancy food, and, for the rest of the trip, try not to gape too much at how the other tenth lives.

So now you know my secret. But if anybody should ask, you didn't read it here, OK?

"The R Rule"

It doesn't make any sense. Whenever they establish something that is supposed to be accessible to people with disabilities but isn't really, they will say: "Well, the disabled person simply has to ask a friend to help out a bit." Whether the plan is for Supermailboxes that people with different impairments can't get to, get the mail out of, or sort; for places with doors that can't be opened by nonambulatory or short statured people, or classes without professional notetakers for participants with hearing or manual impairments; they will blithely wave off any protests by people with disabilities by telling them to just ask a friend to help.

25

But stop and think about that for a minute. Because this is one of those statements that seems solid enough in a dimly-lit room, but under a light begins to decompose.

Imagine that you wear a navy pin-striped suit and Rolex every day to your office on the 24th floor of the banking tower. Who would you think is going to be playing golf with you this weekend? Do you suppose it will be the strawberry-picker who lives in a mobile home in the country? The bearded author of "How Bankers are Destroying You and Me"? The little old lady who hands out *The Watchtower* on the street corner, maybe? Or would you expect it to be some other banker who wears a navy suit and Rolex during the week?

We all tend to have friends with similar lifestyles and outlooks on life to ours. I call this "The Rawnie Rule", or "The R Rule", for short. (I figure if Murphy can have a Law and Peter can have a Principle, I can have a Rule.) According to this Rule, bankers will tend to choose other bankers as friends, students will choose other students, single mothers will choose other single mothers, and people with disabilities, yep, will tend to choose other people with the same disabilities.

I remember the time I arrived at the airport late at night without an attendant. The airport worker who wheeled me down to the baggage area (which they do even if you have your own attendant) was very concerned about this. He asked several times if a friend was meeting me and, when I assured him that a friend was not only meeting me but was bringing along a van with a wheelchair-lift, he let out a big sigh of relief.

Once we reached the baggage area, I had to stifle a giggle when he saw that my friend also used a wheelchair and gulped: "This ...is `your friend'...the one who will take care of you!" It didn't help me keep my composure when my friend whispered, "Who was he expecting—José Canseco?"

Both of the major airlines want someone who can't travel alone to pay 50% extra to take an attendant. But, in my experience, one of the airlines has very specific ideas about just who that attendant should be. Before every flight, this airline would demand my G.P.'s assessment and a resumé of my proposed attendant's qualifications. Then they would leave the final decision up to someone who never even spoke to me about it. No matter how far in advance I submitted this information, though, they would always wait until it was near the date of departure—they even phoned me the night before, once—to reject my attendant. One time, they rejected my son on the basis that he was youngish and wouldn't know what to do to help me. I tried to explain that no one knows the what-to-do's better than someone who's grown up with a disabled person, but they were not impressed. Another time, they rejected my neighbour with the reason that she was bringing her tot and in an emergency might become too upset and abandon me. "Well", I said, "so might the pilot but you're not grounding him". But this didn't move them either. The other major airline, however, seems to believe I know what I'm doing and never questions my choice of attendant.

Once, a friend of mine had no trouble at all getting cleared by the fussy airline because more than a decade ago she had received a degree in Nursing. In fact, an airline worker phoned and congratulated me on finally choosing a "good" attendant. If you keep The R Rule in mind, though, you would not be surprised to learn that my friend, like me, was seriously hearing impaired. We had a lot of fun on that trip. However, you can guess what the trip was like for the airline personnel who tried first to communicate with me and then, in frustration, turned to my attendant. I didn't create a hassle for the airline on purpose, of course; it's just that it was extremely hard to find a friend who fit their particular criteria and wanted to be my attendant on a trip to Ottawa in the middle of winter for nothing.

So, if you have a disability, you should remember The R Rule. Whenever someone tells you to "ask a friend to help", ignore them. Instead, if things have been structured in such a way that you need someone to do something for you, don't ask a friend. Ask a hostile stranger.

Getting There

I could tell she liked me. But then, why wouldn't she? My resumé was so well done: I felt like it should be read aloud to a wildly cheering audience at the Stratford Festival. The lengthy list of all the scholarships and awards I had amassed made the Free Trade Agreement look positively terse. Why wouldn't she—or any employer—like the prospect of hiring me?

She leaned against the edge of the desk and twirled her glasses in one hand while she asked me all the regular job interview questions. Her grin broadened and she even began to nod approvingly as the interview wore on. Best of all, though, she had never given me THE LOOK—you know, that dreadful, sugary "Don't-call-us-dear-we'll-call-you" look which would shutter the eyes of most prospective employers as soon as they glimpsed my wheelchair.

"I couldn't care less what wheels my employees use..." she started to say. `Yup', I thought, excitedly. `This employer is different. She's a real maverick! The type to stride confidently into uncharted waters!'

"...but there are certain standards, you know," she finished as her grin evaporated. `Well, maybe not quite a maverick,' I thought, `and maybe she'd confine her striding to the shallow end of a public swimming pool. But, at least, she'd not succumbed to THE LOOK yet.' I quickly reassured her that a wheelchair does not foreshadow poor attendance or below-average productivity from an employee. In fact, if the officeplace has the few requirements of physical accessibility—as hers already did—the employee who uses a wheelchair expects no special treatment at all. Her grin returned.

"O.K." she said brightly. "The boring part of the interview is over. Now comes the fun part: your responses to specific work situations. You're gonna love this!" I did not share her concept of `fun' but put on an `Oh Boy!' expression anyway.

"Imagine this," she ordered, "It is Friday afternoon and you are working at your desk in our main office when all of a sudden...BANGO!" she slapped her hand against the desk, "...an emergency call comes in from our branch out in Surrey. Three-fourths of their office have gone home sick and they have a major presentation on Monday. They ask you to come help them prepare. What do you do?"

I wanted to say 'Have the place quarantined,' but didn't think that was what she wanted to hear. "I pitch in and help them as soon as possible." I said a little smugly.

"And when would that be?" she asked. "Immediately? Saturday morning? Sunday afternoon?"

"Next Thursday," I replied.

Her grin collapsed as I explained that, since I used a wheelchair and could not drive, I had to use the Parallel Transit System—sometimes called the wheelchair buses. Where I lived, a ride on these buses had to be booked three days in advance but the dispatch office was closed afternoons and weekends. When she started to protest that, "Surely, in a work-related crisis...," I told her about the Friday afternoon I had come down with a five-alarm toothache and learned that even in the heart of a minor medical crisis, the system was inflexible.

She was silent a few seconds then said in a more subdued voice: "Let's go on to the next situation—it's late Friday afternoon again. The report you've been working on for months is due Monday and you are working a bit late in order to wrap it up. Everybody has already stopped off for coffee next door and then headed out. You are just about to leave too when all of a sudden..." she was about to slap her desk again but nervously tucked her hand into a pocket instead "...um...all of a sudden you discover some important information that would change the entire report. What would you do?"

"I wouldn't ever work late," I answered. "Or come early. Or stop for coffee with my colleagues after work. You see, the Parallel Transit System can only book me a ride for when the bus is available. That means, either I go when everybody else on the bus goes or I don't go at all. And they take a dim view of last-minute cancellations," I added darkly.

"Good employees must be responsive to the demands of their work situation," she muttered while putting on her glasses. "They must have a maximum of flexibility." I could feel my throat tightening.

"I could be flexible!" I almost whined. "I couldn't afford this myself, but perhaps if the company could pay for a wheel-chair-accessible taxi to take me to and from the suburb where I live whenever I work late or on weekends or have an unscheduled meeting to attend or..."

"...We're not in the habit of subsidizing public transporta-tion," she snapped. Then she held her hand out to me and thanked me for coming. Clearly, the interview was over.

As I turned to go, she called out, "It was a real pleasure to meet you. Oh, and one last thing: you needn't call us, dear, we'll call you."

MEETINGS & MONSTERS
The Life & Times of
a Disabled Advocate

Rawnie Dunn

Wally The Wicked

You would not be reading this if it weren't for Wally. For years now, Wally has given much of his time to making sure *Transition*, the monthly magazine of the BC Coalition of People with Disabilities is interesting, properly assembled, and on time. But that's not what this story is about. You see, what most people don't know is that deep down good ol', modest, hardworking, dependable Wally has a WICKED sense of humour. But after you're finished reading about the terrible joke he played on me many years ago, you'll know.

It happened back when I was a new Board member attending my very first conference at Naramata, BC. I still felt painfully shy when talking to Board members at meetings but this conference promised to be far more of an ordeal to a Nervous Neurotic like myself as it would be attended by hundreds of total strangers! Being an Anxious Worrier-type, I resolved to spend the weekend being as inconspicuous and agreeable as possible, no matter what! Therefore, I had to get there in the late afternoon in order to melt into the dinnertime crowd. The car I was travelling in left at noon but, unfortunately, it broke down along the way and my driving companions and I arrived just as everyone else was thinking about heading off to bed.

...Yes, Yes, I know. Those of you who know me are scratching your heads and thinking: "Wha-a-at? Nervous Neurotic, Anxious Worrier-type, painfully shy? HER?" Well, all I can say is that people change. Nowadays I have no desire to be either inconspicuous or agreeable; back then, though, it seemed like the greatest crime I could commit was to inconvenience someone. But to get back to the story...

So, there we were; having to rouse the Conference Organizers, the Registration Clerk, the volunteer attendants, and the cook. After registering, a volunteer attendant wheeled me to my assigned room. When we got there, we found the room had only two beds, a single and a double, with suitcases already on both beds.

"Gee!" the volunteer said, "They must expect you to share the double bed with another woman. Want to go back and complain?"

This was horrible! Did they really suppose I'd be willing to share a bed—even if it were a large one? Were they SERI-

OUS? Were they even SANE? I wanted to storm back to Reception. However, the prospect of making a scene at the Registration Desk was intimidating. The other woman sharing the bed was probably cool about this, I thought, and I would look like a real jerk if I made a fuss. I imagined people pointing to me all weekend and whispering: 'Not only is she a BOTHER, but she's a LAH-DEE-DAH ONE, too!'

I tried to look laid-back as I dumped my suitcase on the other side of the bed and said, "Nah, this is no big deal. Besides, I heard they were overbooked; they probably haven't got another space, anyhow." But I tried to make the room less foreign by laying out my favourite nightie—an ego-boosting froufrou of red satin and lace—on my side of the bed.

Then we hurried back to the kitchen where the cook had prepared supper for the latecomers.

A small crowd had gathered in the kitchen. Two tables had been set up for the diners while a circle of friends, sympathizers, and curiosity-seekers surrounded the tables. I wheeled up to a table and quietly started working through the lasagna.

Suddenly there was a tremendous crash! Every head jerked around to look at the floor by my feet where my suitcase had been tossed. Above me, wearing an expression like an alligator might have at a handbag store, loomed Wally.

"I am only going to say this ONCE," he hissed.

Then raising his voice and stabbing the air in front of me with his finger, he continued slowly and loudly, "GET...OUT...OF...MY...BED...AND...STAY...OUT!"

36

Then he dropped my red nightie onto my lap and stomped out of the kitchen.

The rest of the weekend was a nightmare. No amount of whimpering could convince Wally that it wasn't my fault! The Registration Clerk assured me that they would NEVER knowingly book two people—even of the same gender—into the same bed and quickly reassigned me, but Wally continued to treat me like I was a Mad Marauder. If I happened to be in the cafeteria line behind him, he would roll his eyes and say in a booming voice:

"OH GEEZ! SHE'S FOLLOWING ME AGAIN!"

If I entered a workshop in which he was sitting, he'd bellow:

"WILL SHE NEVER LEAVE ME ALONE?"

All my plans for the weekend evaporated. It is difficult to be 'inconspicuous and pleasant', you know, when someone acts like you are a cross between Jack-the-Ripper and poison oak!

The sun shone fiercely on the morning everybody was supposed to leave Naramata. I came to breakfast late in order to get an empty table by the window and sit with its warming rays on my back as I ate. Suddenly, I was in shadow. I looked up and cringed because outlined against the sunlight, like a dinosaur-bird with folded wings, was Wally.

"I'd like to say one last thing to you," he began sternly. "The NEXT TIME you are booked into MY ROOM at a conference..."

Then he dropped his voice and grinned.

"...leave it that way, hmm?"

He walked away, chortling to himself. I'm sure he was thinking he'd pulled off a great practical joke that weekend. He probably still does. But then, I did manage to get you to read the whole story, didn't I? And what is that thing they say about "he who laughs last"?

Cold

Sometimes we Vancouverites forget just how lucky we are. Last November I was reminded of that fact when I attended a Council of Canadians with Disabilities (CCD) Executive Meeting in Winnipeg. As a child I had lived in Winnipeg but over the years Winnipeg's winters had taken on the mythical status of such things as UFOs, ghosts, and Yetis. Vancouver's tepid version of winter has spoilt us Vancouverites to the point where we assume cold is something that is felt only at ski resorts on holiday weekends and is accompanied by mugs of hot cocoa in front of a fire.

Nevertheless, for my trip to Winnipeg, I had been persuaded to borrow a voluminous poncho overcoat that would convert into a tent that sleeps six. Along with the fur mitts, scarves, socks, and underwear, I thought I'd be prepared for the worst Mother Nature could throw at me.

When the bus driver first wheeled me out of the Winnipeg airport, however, I remembered the real meaning of the word "winter". In Winnipeg, "winter" is when the snow is so thickly piled up the sides of the buildings that they look like igloos and all the traffic signs like ice sculptures; when the breath you take into your nostrils puts you into a state of shock; when your nose, cheeks, and fingers turn shades of red and blue bright enough to decorate a Christmas tree. I tucked myself into my poncho and ignored the passersby staring at the odd sight of a whimpering tent on wheels.

Once in town, it soon became obvious that the Council of Canadians with Disabilities' National Coordinator was a vicious sadist. (Otherwise, why would he have scheduled a meeting in Winnipeg in late November—even if CCD's national headquarters IS there?) When he presented us with the weekend's agenda, we were stunned to discover that not only must the workday begin at 8:30 a.m. on both Saturday and Sunday, but he had cunningly contrived the meeting to be held in a building a few blocks away. As the building was "too close to take a bus to", we had to take to the streets before there was even the chance of a thaw. Diabolical, eh?

The biggest surprise for me, though, was the reactions of the other representatives who were from Alberta, Saskatchewan, Quebec, Nova Scotia, and Newfoundland. While my bones and teeth were making enough noise inside my porta-tent to background a Mariachi Band, these people were actually smiling at each other. Our Chairperson was by far the worst of them. In weather so cold that I wouldn't subject my frozen foods to it, she stood in an open coat and, squinting up at where the sun should have been, crowed about what a "beautiful day" it was! (Mind you, she's from Alberta and everybody knows Albertans are a little strange. I mean, who else but those Albertans would have created that Yuppie Disneyland, the West Edmonton Mall?)

It felt like years passed there, but it was actually only a few days before I flew home to Vancouver to recover. I've been back in Vancouver just over two months but already the memory of that pitiless cold is starting to fade, like all nightmares do.

Today, as I write, the Vancouver sun is shining yet again, dogs are lazily sunning on their lawns, and some people are wandering outside in their shirt sleeves. Just yesterday I noticed that the blood is starting to return to my right leg again. Hopefully, I shall be entirely thawed out in time for the meeting in Ottawa this February. I'm really looking forward to it. According to the travel brochures, winters in Eastern Canada are even milder than Vancouver ones.

The Haunted
Shower-Room

PART I

One balmy night in mid-March, a few years ago, I decided to take a bath. There was nothing—I hasten to add—unusual about this. I have gleefully paid homage to this form of godliness countless times. In fact, this would not have been remarkable at all if I hadn't been at a DisAbled Women's Network of BC (DAWN BC) conference at the time. Bathtubs and I have a long history of mishaps. Normally, I wouldn't even consider climbing into a tub late at night with no one around but, you see, this one talked.

Oh, all right, it didn't exactly talk. It sang. Every time I passed it, a melody like the refrain from Swan Lake wafted out of the shower-room. It wasn't until after I had actually passed the room a few times, that it started to talk:

"Hey, you..." it said in a whisper.

"Leave me alone!" I hissed. "I don't talk to bathtubs."

"No need to be hostile!" it whined. "I just wanted to invite you to come see the shower-room."

I hesitated. "Well, I guess it wouldn't hurt to just look..."

So, I entered the shower-room. Someone had recently taken a shower and steam swirled around my feet like something out of a "Twilight Zone" episode. The entire room glistened in the moonlight.

As if on cue, my back and shoulders began to ache and spasms crept up my legs. The bleak threat of another sleepless night stretched out before me. Yet here, I thought, was the Magic Antidote. I let myself believe that after an hour's soak in very hot water, my muscles would smooth out like butter on a sunny windowsill. Never mind that my attendant had fallen asleep in the lounge, never mind that I was carrying a load of laundry on my lap, and never mind that the bathtub seemed unusually deep. I told myself that the solution to all my problems—if not to all the World's problems, too—was no farther away than the flick of a faucet with an 'H' on it.

I threw my laundry onto the floor beside the tub, and, with a squeal of joy, scrambled into the tub as it filled.

A little later, the water was turning cold. 'Time to get out of the tub, dry off, and get to bed!', I told myself. Unfortunately, this was more easily said than done. Every time I grabbed the grab bars and tried to slide myself up the side of the tub, I only managed to get within an inch of the top where I would hover for a moment before sliding down again. Several times I tried, but the tub had become a porcelain Mount Everest.

Screaming didn't help. Thirty minutes, then sixty, then ninety passed. I grabbed whatever laundry I could see through the tangle of hair in front of my eyes and put it on. As I sat there in my purple jacket, red toque, and green socks, I began to fear that I might never be rescued; that I might be discovered someday in the distant future as an archaeological curiosity that had petrified in mid-shiver. The shower-room seemed to be a white-tiled tomb, and the tub a coffin.

Suddenly, I became aware of someone giggling. I looked up and saw three women standing there trying to suppress their amusement. In that moment, I realized that what had seemed like High Tragedy only seconds before, was actually more like Theatre of the Absurd and started giggling myself. When I came to breakfast the next morning, everyone teased me about the incident. It wasn't long before I was sick of hearing shower-room jokes. But worse was yet to come...

The Haunted
Shower-Room
PART II

The next year, the DisAbled Women's Network of BC again held its annual conference at the same place. My friends were still smirking, warning me to stay away from the shower-room, but this was easy to do as it wasn't singing anymore. Three days passed without it making a sound. Then, on the last night, it happened. I was passing the shower-room alone when out floated that eerie Swan Lake refrain. I froze. Then a voice whispered my name.

"Give it up right now!" I almost screamed. "There is no way I'm getting into that tub again! So just forget it!"

"Calm down," purred the voice. "I wasn't even going to suggest it. I guess you haven't noticed that there's something new here this year. Something that will prevent you from getting stuck again. Something that is the solution to all your problems, to all your dreams. But I guess you are not interested..."

"You got that right!" I spluttered, as I turned to wheel away. Then I paused. "But, uh, just for the sake of, you know, conversation, er ...just what is this, um, `thing', anyhow?"

The voice then drew my attention to an enourmous metal chair sitting in the corner of the bathroom. It looked like something out of a plumber's nightmare. Pipes went in every direction and had been welded together in welt-like seams. The rubber on the rear wheels seemed to have been sprayed on and the front wheels were crooked. The monster was coated in flesh-coloured pink paint which had chipped away in places revealing an undercoat of putrid green. It was probably the ugliest chair I have ever encountered but when I saw the words FOR SHOWER-ROOM USE on its back, it couldn't have been more enchanting if it had been a throne from the Taj Mahal.

All my friends would have teased me if they saw me going into the shower-room, though, so I returned to my bedroom and waited until after the hall lights had been turned off before wheeling down to the shower-room.

When I transferred into the shower-chair I almost rolled right out again, as it was lopsided. It was also awkward to move as both wheels would not always make contact with the floor at the same time. Nevertheless, while clutching an extra-large man-sized shirt and gumboots which would serve as housecoat and slippers, I eventually maneuvered it into the shower-room.

The shower was hot and soothing. Maybe even more wonderful than the water, however, was the feeling that I—clever and resourceful creature that I am—was getting away with something. 'Ah yes,' I was going to say to myself with a half-smile whenever someone joked about last year's mishap, 'you may giggle, my friend, but I have the last laugh!'

When the shower was over, I put on my shirt and boots and tried to wheel back out the shower-room door. It was tough. After several tries, the chair was finally on the crest of the doorsill—where it stopped. I tried rocking it, pulling against the door jamb, reaching down to adjust the casters, shifting my weight, pushing against the floor with my boots, and beating it, but it wouldn't budge. I thought I heard the faint sound of laughter and glared suspiciously at the bathtub.

'My friends will never let me live this down', I groaned. An image flashed through my mind of me wearing a card on which were the words SHOWER-ROOM in a red circle with a diagonal line across it. 'No! No one will ever know that it has happened again,' I vowed. I decided to wait until someone passed the shower-room and then, feigning an urge to shake her hand—maybe both her hands—haul myself towards her. That way, I figured, nobody would be the wiser!

Ten minutes passed. After another ten minutes I decided to speed things up by making a few casual-sounding noises. No response. The noises got louder and louder. By the time they sounded like full-blown hysteria, one of the new board members ran into the bathroom.

I could hardly believe my luck for I knew that she was a sensitive and discreet woman and would keep this a secret. Then, behind her, I saw another board member, a woman with a notorious sense of humour. This second woman wordlessly grabbed the chair and wheeled me out of the bathroom into the lounge, where a party was in progress. There, I was forced to sit—wearing a housecoat and slipper set that looked like it had come from the fashion pages of *Auto Mechanic Digest*—in the centre of a gaggle of laughing women. As if this weren't enough, doors started opening down the hall and others peered out to see what all the noise was about. One woman even laughingly threatened to get her camera. All I could do was sit there and whimper.

And so, dear reader, there is a lesson to be learned from all this. For your sake, I fervently pray that you heed it well. Please remember this: if, on some night when the wind softly rustles through the trees and the full moon casts a ghostly pallor over the land, you think you hear a haunting melody drifting out of the shower-room at a DAWN BC Conference—BEWARE!

Visions & Hallucinations

I t was one of the best times of my life. It was unique, informative, stimulating, and well-organized; it was both philosophical and action-oriented, and most of all—it was fun! But it ended in the worst way possible.

"IT" was the second National Educational Association of Disabled Students (NEADS) conference, "Visions", held in St. John's, Newfoundland. I learned a lot at that Conference—not only about the issues, but about the people there, too.

I learned a lot about how translation for the hearing impaired works. There were many translators at the Conference with various specialties: some specialized in Oral Translation with no signing, some specialized in ASL, others in Sign English. The two translators who were assigned to me specialized in Patience. As I'm still learning sign language, they would do a kind of simplified version of it with considerable instant-replays. As well, because the same lack of co-ordination of my muscles which causes me to use a wheelchair also makes it hard for my eyes to focus steadily on details more than five or six feet away, they would have to sit facing me with our knees almost touching.

The day the Conference ended started nicely enough. Two friends I'd met at the Conference and I rented a white New Yorker so we could do a little impromptu sightseeing before we left Newfoundland. I stretched out in the back seat while the driver and the navigator took their positions in front. Although I couldn't carry on a conversation in that situation, I did hear some things they said. Specifically, I heard them say, "Thank goodness she can't hear us and doesn't know how lost we are!" (Actually, I'd already figured that out after we spent 15 minutes roaming around and around in a shopping mall parking lot.) That, though, was pleasant compared to what followed.

Even when the Custom Transit van took off for the airport and left me hollering on the sidewalk, it was tolerable. Before he left the driver came up to me to explain why he was not taking me but, as I couldn't hear what he was saying due to all the traffic around us, this wasn't very reassuring. I mean, for all I knew he could have said: "I'm abandoning you here, because I WANT to!"

At the airport, the baggage clerk kept passing me notes which said things like "Please show me your ticket." and "Is this your baggage?" This surprised me as I can essentially hear well enough to function at a quiet ticket counter. It eventually dawned on me that the airline personnel thought I was deaf. I was about to correct them when I remembered how deaf people say they are treated differently from hard-of-hearing people, so I decided to take my hearing aids out and see what I could learn.

When it was time to board the aircraft, about an hour later, I discovered that they had already told the Flight Attendants that I was deaf, so I decided to continue in this fashion until we changed planes in Montreal.

In Montreal, however, the plane we were supposed to change to needed repairs so I kept it up (or rather, them out) almost five hours more. In a way, though, I was glad. I had heard many hair-raising rumours about Montrealers getting mad at anglo-Canadians who butchered the French language whenever they spoke it. At least, I thought, they will not expect me to converse—maybe they will even think I'm a francophone deaf person! I spent the time trying intently to look like a Montrealer who had just come to meet someone. (This is a hard thing to do when your wheelchair has 'St. John's to Vancouver' airline stickers plastered all over it.)

Even when the plane landed in Vancouver, I still had to travel for almost an hour before I finally entered the front door of my place—seventeen and a half hours after I left the Conference. I have never been so totally, semi-consciously, spine-crushingly exhausted. By that time, I was having a few "visions" of my own.

So, will I want to go to the next National Educational Association of Disabled Students conference? Of course, but I do hope I can cut down on the travelling next time. What do you think are the chances of having it at my house?

The Weekend
Of The Living Dead

The very last disability they will acknowledge will be fatigue. "What do you mean?" I can hear them cry in protest. "We've acknowledged fatigue for ages! We always include it in our lists of disabilities and we urge other people to consider it when employing, training, or transporting disabled people... it's just that, uh, we don't actually, you know, do anything about it ourselves or, maybe, give it a second thought when, er, planning or using or, well, um..."

Who are "they"? Well, sometimes, "they" are us. As a low-energy person who goes to every conference of every self-help group I'm invited to (and even some I'm not wanted at) I'm able to say how various groups rate in the books of the Bombed-Out. Although I respect and admire self-help groups for people with disabilities for always considering the needs of people with visual, hearing, or mobility impairments, I'd have to rate their get-togethers amongst the worst I've ever numbed my way through for the way they ignore the needs of those with Staying-Awake impairments. The worst of the worst—alas—is my favourite, the Council of Canadians with Disabilities (CCD) at which I—double alas—spent many years on their National Council.

CCD Council meetings always started a.s.a.p. after my plane touched down in whatever city the meeting was being held in. When I straggled into that evening's Council meeting, feeling like the Scarecrow before Dorothy stuffed the straw back into him, a voice would come over the loudspeakers reprimanding latecomers and insisting that we be at the board-room table all bright-eyed, bushy-tailed, and ready-to-go at nine o'clock the next morning.

The next morning my alarm would go off at five o'clock and I'd lie in bed twenty minutes trying to threaten myself into getting up. The sandman comes every night to most people to sprinkle sand in the corners of their eyes. When he comes to me, though, he applies Krazy Glue to my back and I can wrench myself out of bed only by leaving behind the part of my brain that focuses my eyes and co-ordinates my lips, teeth, and tongue when I speak.

It didn't seem to matter how early I got up: I could never find the time for a nourishing breakfast. So I would spend the first part of the meeting staring at the coffee table. At lunch,

I crashed on the nearest level surface that I cold find. A good friend on the CCD staff would sneak me a plate of goodies when the meeting started again and I'd try to crunch away at it while ignoring the hostile glances I kept getting from other Council members. When the meeting was over, I'd go back up to my room and sleep face down with all my clothes on until midnight. Then I got up and got ready for bed. At five o'clock, everything was the same as the day before. Only worse.

After one especially arduous Council meeting, I learned I was going to fly home by Executive Class. 'Bigger seats, more legroom: I can SLEEP!' I thought ecstatically. When I was finally on the plane home I snuggled amongst the two dozen pillows I'd asked for and closed my eyes with a sigh. 'CCD is getting nice', I told myself. 'Why, they've even given us these neat little red CCD pins!'

"What is THIS?" I heard the man in the seat next to me ask.

'Oh oh.' I thought, 'He's probably asking the Fight Attendant if there's some kind of pillow-shaped mold growing in the seat beside him.' I opened my eyes and saw a friendly executive-type eyeing my CCD pin. I explained pleasantly but briefly about the Council of Canadians with Disabilities and was about to close my eyes again when he said, "Really? I troubleshoot for a multinational corporation and they are always interested in this kind of thing. I'd like to be able to say something to them but I don't know much about it."

Fighting back my tears, I put on my best CCD rep smile and played ambassador for the rest of the trip. Sometimes I'm so responsible it's sickening.

Eventually, the flight was over and I was being wheeled around the Vancouver airport. At least I thought it was Vancouver Airport. By that time, I wouldn't have known or cared if we had landed somewhere in Iraq. My mind, my eyes, my hearing, my sense of touch, and my body muscles had all faded away. The only thing left of me was this big smile. I felt, and probably looked, like a disabled Cheshire cat.

A fellow disability advocate was there.

"Well, hi!" he exclaimed. Fortunately, my grin was still in place.

"CCD?" he asked, and took my grin to be an affirmative response.

"Boy," he said, "are you ever smart. Here the rest of us are slaving for the movement while you're out travelling and taking holidays!"

I wanted to bash him a good one but my arms wouldn't work. All I could manage in reply was that silly grin.

In summary, the needs of the Chronically Beat are as urgent as the needs of people with visual impairments, or wheelchair-users, or deaf people. But although a conference would be (and should be) unthinkable without tapes, accessible washrooms, and sign language interpreters, it is often forgotten that breaks and rest periods are important, too. But if I protest, the response is: "We'd like to accommodate people like you, Rawnie, but it would cost us just too much time and money."

Gee, why does that argument have such a familiar ring to it?

ENDANGERED GENDERS

Separating the Women from the Men

Vive La Différence

As Dorothy Parker once said: "The disabled men, they are not like you and me." Well O.K., the original quote is really about "The Rich", but it's the paraphrased quote that I hear said again and again. Sometimes I hear it said with hands thrown in the air in a gesture of exasperation, sometimes it's said with a snarl, sometimes with a leer. However it's said, though, it's something of a truism for disabled women. Still, there is a bit of resistance to the formation of disabled women's groups and we are often told that we should all cooperate exclusively within Disabled Persons' organizations.

Well, I don't know about you, but I'm getting mighty tired of being a "person". I mean, although I am quite happy to be called a "disabled person" sometimes, I am first and foremost a woman. The term "person", however, is androgynous and tends to make one forget that we actually come in two (very) different genders.

Fact is, our society is gender-mad. Places like shoe stores, washrooms, and beer parlour entrances are different for men and women. Even when we wear identical shirts we're supposed to do the buttons up on opposite sides. And come to think about it, when was the last time you encountered a beer ad aimed at Persons? Or an ad for perfume? Or Cigarettes? Life insurance? Deodorant? Motorcycles? Frozen dinners? Even recruiting ads talk about "the men and women" in the armed forces—not the "persons".

The rules of the gender-game are pretty wonky, all right, and a lot of changes are in order. Many men are fed up with the conventional macho, non-fathering role and most women detest the dithery role that's been delivered to them. But "persons" aren't even invited to play!

"Persons" really exist only in Law Books but, with respect to "the disabled", the word has slid into fanatically popular use in everyday life, too. A while ago, I asked a group of able-bodied students to substitute the phrase "disabled men and women" for "disabled persons" every time they discussed us in class. Nobody did this, though. Not even once. Later, one of the students told me that it wasn't just that she kept forgetting to do this but that the idea also made her vaguely uncomfortable. I think she was onto something there. "Persons" is the natural term for a society to use which doesn't think of disabled individuals as sexual beings. Disabled women's groups not only challenge the stereotype of disabled people as asexual, they also deal with the needs and experiences that are a consequence of a disabled woman's sexuality.

I remember, soon after my son was born, going to the maternity ward and gazing at all the newborns through the window. Newborns are really pretty much alike—even as a proud new mother I had to admit that everybody looked like Winston Churchill having a temper tantrum to me—but there they were: row upon row of them snuggly wrapped up in either blue or pink blankets with cards joyously proclaiming I'M A BOY! or I'M A GIRL! stuck to the head of each plexiglass bassinet. One poor soul, though, was wrapped in a yellow blanket and had no card announcing its gender. It must have been a Person.

Tell Them I'm A Duck
...a radio play for six women

CAST OF CHARACTERS:

> NON-DISABLED FEMALE REPORTER
> NON-DISABLED FEMALE PASSER-BY
> NON-DISABLED POOR WOMAN
> DISABLED PASSER-BY/EVE
> DISABLED MOTHER/ANN, HOLDING INFANT
> WOMAN WITH A HIDDEN DISABILITY

REPORTER: Today, the "Trivia News Team" is on the street in front of the Post Office to find out what the average woman-in-the-street thinks of the present Postal Service. [footsteps] Here comes someone now... Excuse me, ma'am...

NON-DISABLED FEMALE PASSER-BY: Yes?

REPORTER: "Trivia News" would like to know what you, as the average-woman-in-the-street, think of the present Postal Service.

NON-DISABLED FEMALE PASSER-BY: Well, it's an intriguing operation, really. It has had a history of labour troubles, but you must look at them within the context of the entire labour struggle while keeping in mind the complicated background of Canadian...

REPORTER: [interrupts] Well, there you have it! A first-hand account of the anger and hatred the present Postal Service arouses. [Footsteps] Here comes someone else. Excuse me, ma'am...

POOR WOMAN: Whaddya want?

REPORTER: "Trivia News" would like to know what you, as the average-woman-in-the-street, think about the present Postal Service.

POOR WOMAN: Don't know really. Never used the Postal Service.

REPORTER: You've never mailed a letter?

POOR WOMAN: Nope.

REPORTER: I understand. You are so filled with anger about the present Service that your anger is retroactive.

POOR WOMAN: Nope.

REPORTER: Oh. Well then I guess it's because of the insufficient number of mailboxes. You've never been able to find one.

POOR WOMAN: Nope.

REPORTER: Oh. Can't stand the possibility that your mail might be tampered with?

POOR WOMAN: Can't afford a stamp.

REPORTER: Oh, I see. You're poverty-stricken. Well, I'm sorry, but "Trivia News" doesn't want your opinion. We're after the opinion of the average woman-in-the-street and you're not the average woman.

POOR WOMAN: Wanna bet? [footsteps leaving]

[brief pause]

REPORTER: Now, here's an unexpected development! You folks at home can't see this but someone in a wheelchair is coming up to me, for an undetermined reason.

FEMALE DISABLED PASSERBY: Hi! I'd like to express my thoughts on the Postal Service...

REPORTER: ...I'm sorry. "Trivia News" doesn't want your opinion.

DISABLED PASSERBY: Because I'm not 'average'?

REPORTER: Because you're not a woman.

DISABLED PASSERBY: So what am I? A duck?

REPORTER: Look, everyone knows there are three genders: "male" which includes everyone that's male, "female" which includes everyone that's female, and "persons" which includes everyone that's disabled! I mean, in all the really modern buildings there are always three washrooms: men, women, and wheelchairs, O.K.?

DISABLED PASSERBY: Hey, wait a minute! Not all disabled women use wheelchairs, you know! Some of us can't hear or can't see. Some have hidden disabilities like epilepsy. Or learning disabilities. Or mental disabilities. Or psychiatric disabilities. Sometimes, just being a woman in this society is a handicap!

REPORTER: Don't tell ME about being a woman in this society! I know ALL about that! I belong to a REAL big women's group and we don't EVER talk about disabilities—we don't even have any disabled members! SO THERE!

DISABLED PASSERBY: Do you have an accessible washroom at your meeting-place?

REPORTER: Well, we use an old building and, uh...

DISABLED PASSERBY: Do you have a Telecommunications Device for the Deaf?

REPORTER: Uh, I don't know what...

DISABLED PASSERBY: Do you advertise in newsletters or at places which disabled women use a lot?

REPORTER: Gee, I guess we never...

DISABLED PASSERBY: Don't you think that might have something to do with why you don't have any disabled members?

REPORTER: Well, we're talking about a Woman's Group—not a hospital! You disabled people lead different lives. Separate lives. Separate but equal, of course. I understand your problems, really I do. I think you're all very brave. I care. I mean, I gave to the last Telethon, you know.

DISABLED PASSERBY: Quack, quack.

REPORTER: No, really! I think it's just astounding to see all the incredible feats you people do. You people are really more able than we are. Things that would be impossible for someone like me to do, you people do all the time. For you, though, the impossible just takes a little longer.

DISABLED PASSERBY: The impossible is just plain impossible. But a lot of things wouldn't be impossible if there weren't so many barriers in our society. One of which is stereotypical thinking like yours...

REPORTER: ...Well, you folks-at-home are hearing quite a drama today and... My goodness! Here comes another person in a wheelchair! It looks like they are going to speak to each other...

DISABLED MOTHER: [to DISABLED PASSERBY] Eve! I haven't seen you for a long time!

EVE [formerly DISABLED PASSERBY]: [to DISABLED MOTHER] Too long, Ann! How are you and the baby?

[baby cries]

REPORTER: Ann, is that a baby you're holding? My goodness, it is! Who does it belong to? Who is the mother?

MOTHER: I am. [to EVE] So, Eve, you were going to tell me how things have been going for you and...uh...uh...

EVE: Adam.

REPORTER: [to MOTHER] Who's Adam? Your husband, Ann?

MOTHER: I don't have a husband now.

REPORTER: I'm so sorry, dear.

MOTHER: I don't WANT a husband now.

REPORTER: Oh.

MOTHER: Adam is Eve's boyfriend.

EVE: He's a disabled man. We're both wheelchair-users.

REPORTER: How cute!

EVE: Cute?

REPORTER: I mean, naturally, you're both disabled, Eve.

EVE: My former boyfriend wasn't disabled, although I was.

REPORTER: How tragic!

EVE: I give up!

[Baby starts to hiccup]

MOTHER: [burping baby] There, there...

EVE: [to MOTHER] Ann, you look beat. Let's go for a cup of coffee at the cafe on the corner.

REPORTER: [to MOTHER] Don't go yet, Ann! I wanted to ask you some questions, like 'Who is your nurse?'

MOTHER: I don't have a nurse.

REPORTER: Then who takes care of you?

MOTHER: Who do you think? [baby starts hiccuping again]. Look, I gotta go now. [EVE and MOTHER chatter together briefly in the background as they exit.]

REPORTER: Well, folks-at-home, I guess the baby does. [footsteps] Here comes another woman. Excuse me, ma'am, "Trivia News" would like to know...

WOMAN: No, it wouldn't. You yourself just said so.

REPORTER: I don't understand. You don't use a wheel-chair.

WOMAN: Nevertheless, I am also a disabled woman.

REPORTER: What is this? A convention? You're every-where today!

WOMAN: I've got a news flash for you: we were always everywhere. We are over 18% of the female population. Just because you don't notice us, doesn't mean we're not there, you know. Just because you don't understand our issues, doesn't mean they don't exist. Sure, we're disabled "persons" too, but we're not genderless, you know.

REPORTER: Well, folks, I guess that about wraps up another "Trivia News" first. I guess we've learned a valuable lesson today. We've learned to stop thinking in terms of three genders: men, women, and persons. From now on, we should remember disabled women: the fourth gender.

WOMAN: [while walking away] Quack, quack, quack, quack, quack!

How It Feels
To Have Spinocerebellar
Degeneration

I was once asked to write something about how it feels to
have my kind of Muscular Dystrophy, but found that it's an
overwhelmingly large question. The only way I can possibly
tackle it is to break it up into small bits, like this...

Rawnie Dunn

HOW IT FEELS TO HAVE S.C.D. AT 7:30 A.M.

Sometimes it feels like I've spent every morning of my life getting kids ready for school. The scenes—lost homework, tantrums over unappetizing lunches, feigned illnesses, notes which they forgot to give me earlier from their teachers demanding that the children wear full costume to a school play rehearsal that morning, or testily saying that the teachers want an emergency meeting with me (to discuss perpetually lost homework or not providing the kids with school play costumes) etc.—are so familiar now that I just sleepily call out one of my stock replies like: "All right, so-never-eat-another-peanut-butter-sandwich-as-long-as-you-live then, but-I-still-refuse-to-cater-to-you-at-school-with-hot-cheese-burgers!" or "I-don't-care-if-you-think-you've-probably-got-typhoid-fever,-smallpox,-and-a-hangnail-today, you're-going-to-school-anyway!" and hope it's appropriate. I guess these scenes haven't much to do with my disability, but they are all I think about in the early morning.

Years ago, when I had a full-time job, we were enacting versions of these scenes as I took them to the daycare at the bottom of the block. I remember the screaming and hollering (theirs) and whining and moaning (mine) that went on as I tried to stop their constant battling. I would pull one child up to either side of my wheelchair when I started to roll down the hill to the daycare. Women in curlers were always peering out of their bedroom windows to see what all the racket was about. I remember wishing that I didn't use a wheelchair then, as my head was smack-dab between their flailing lunchkits and little fists. Other than that, though, I don't recall really thinking about 'how it feels.'

HOW IT FEELS TO HAVE S.C.D. AT 9:00 A.M.

Nowadays, at 9 a.m. I am mostly trying to eat the remains of the kids' cold, mushy breakfast while I write. Again, I don't think much about my disability. Eight years ago, though, something happened which made me think a lot about it. The daycare I used then was—like most of them still are—inaccessible to wheelchair-users, so I'd wait at the foot of the outside steps for the Supervisor to bring out the "Sign-in" book in order for me to sign the kids in. Then I'd wait for the "Wheelchair Van" to come take me to work. One morning, the van arrived before I'd signed the book and the driver bellowed: "Would someone bring the book outside, please? We got an invalid here!" The Supervisor rushed out with the book and I signed it. Then the healthy women in curlers crawled back into bed while the invalid went to work.

HOW IT FEELS TO HAVE S.C.D. AT 4:30 P.M.

At that time in the afternoon, things have finally slowed down enough for me to indulge in a little introspection. However, I'm afraid I am still unable to tell you what S.C.D. feels like, as at 4:30 p.m. I am always sound asleep. If I'm lucky, I'm in bed; if I'm not, I'm at a meeting sitting upright and answering questions—but sound asleep nonetheless.

HOW IT FEELS TO HAVE S.C.D. AT 7:00 P.M.

This is our family time. After an hour of peeling, chopping, boiling, and listening to the children's loving comments: "Not another one of your inedible inventions!" and "Yuk! It smells like it's burnt!" I often end up at the phone ordering pizza (because they're right).

HOW IT FEELS TO HAVE S.C.D. AT 11:00 P.M.

Exactly the same as it does at 4:30 p.m.

It's turning out to be impossible to answer the question at the head of this article in this way. Being a member of our society, I can only really answer that question in terms of how it feels to have S.C.D. while interacting with others. For example: when I'm shopping with a friend and a sales clerk ignores me and asks my friend what I want, or when somebody openly expresses their pity to my children because their mother is disabled, or when someone on the phone becomes impatient with my speech impairment and tells me to phone back after I've sobered up, THEN I know how it feels to have Spinocerebellar Degeneration. It feels awful.

'THEM & US'?
To Non-disabled Friends

"Unable to bathe or get out of bed, Munro, 40, has slowly suffered the horrendous experience of moving from <u>the world of the able-bodied to the world of disabled people</u>." ("Breaking Down Some Barriers", *THE OTTAWA CITIZEN,* May 30, 1988, p. D1) [my underlining]

Rawnie Dunn

The Danger Zone

In every friendship between a non-disabled and a disabled person, there comes a time when the non-disabled friend stops seeing the disabled person's disability.

"Gee," they will say when this happens with me, "I keep forgetting you use a wheelchair and speechread because I don't think of you as a disabled person anymore." Then they will smile broadly as if they have just said something wonderful and can't understand why I've turned the colour of the underbelly of a fish. Somehow, society seems to have the notion that a disability is a BAD THING and the biggest compliment one can give is to ignore it completely.

I have been 'complimented' like this several times by friends who imagine that treating a person with a disability 'like everybody else' means ignoring their special needs. I have gone to many a sleep-over and discovered that my bed was a mattress on the floor with no grab bars around. I have often been invited to an exciting event the next day by friends who forget that Customs Transit must be booked far in advance, and, many times, have had friends say something profound and soul-searching to me while I was turned away which they would laughingly refuse to repeat when I faced them.

The back of my closet is full of such compliments. The alarm clock Max gave me is there. Max always acted like I'd be flattered whenever he forgot about my hearing impairment. The clock he gave me touted a special alarm which promised that it wouldn't "haul you out of bed by your nerves." Unfortunately, it never hauled me out of bed at all and I missed four classes, two Custom Transit rides, and my child's Christmas Concert before it could be replaced.

Also in the back of my closet is the jogging outfit my brother gave me one Christmas. It came complete with a sweatband and sneakers. It was a lovely gesture but probably the most inappropriate gift a wheelchair-user could ever receive. The jumpsuit was a one-piecer with a short zipper at the neck and nowhere else—if you catch my meaning. The washroom was the only place I did anything resembling jogging in it.

Beats me why people think I will be pleased to hear that they have forgotten about my disability. I mean, suppose I pushed myself away from their table, stood up, and fell flat on my face because I forgot I used a wheelchair. Suppose I showed up at their parties without my hearing aids because I forgot I had a hearing impairment. Would they really be that pleased?

The other day, a new friend handed me a heaping platter of spaghetti.

"I forgot about your co-ordination problem," she explained as she helped me pick the noodles and tomatoes out of my hair. "I guess our friendship has entered a Phase of Equality," she said.

I don't call it a Phase of Equality. I call it The Danger Zone.

"A Guide To Sentences And Phrases"

When you have a disability there are certain phrases that you hear over and over again. These sayings are repeated so often that they have formed a kind of Folklore of Disability. Like most folklore, though, they often seem to say one thing but mean something quite different. In order to understand what is meant the next time you hear one of these phrases, the following is offered as a guide to the real meaning of some of the phrases that you, as a person with a disability, can expect to hear...

77

"CONFINED TO A WHEELCHAIR FOR LIFE"

An unfortunate phrase. Wheelchairs are simply tools that can be used by people with mobility-impairments to get around more easily, but this phrase can frighten impressionable people (like me) into imagining that if a wheelchair is sat upon even briefly two gigantic metal arms are going to snake out from under the seat and "confine" the unlucky individual FOR LIFE! I resisted using a wheelchair for years because I was afraid that once "confined" to it I would have to haul it into bed with me.

Even the somewhat milder phrase "IN a wheelchair" bothers me. Mostly because it's not true. Once when I thought I overheard a friend saying to someone else that I was "in a wheelchair", I bellowed "No I'm not! I'm in the can!" My accuracy wasn't too appreciated on that occasion.

"YOU CAN DO ANYTHING!"

Sounds like something that should be set to music, doesn't it? A statement that full of confidence in you can leave you breathlessly planning to sell your life story to a TV-Movie-Of-The-Week. Wait, though. This statement is full of it, all right, but what it's full of is not confidence. The easiest way to understand the real meaning behind this phrase is to add the two words "by yourself" to the end of it. Quite simply, what it means is "Go ahead and do it if you want to, but you won't get any help from me."

"DISABLED PEOPLE ARE MORE CHEERFUL/ACCEPTING/LOVING"

This is a multiple-choice phrase. You get to insert any word from the above selection of "cheerful", "accepting", and "loving". Not that it matters, though, because they all come out to about the same thing. What this phrase means is that not only do you have special physical/mental characteristics, you also have special personal characteristics.

It is probably supposed to be a compliment but it can seem rather intimidating. Surely, no reasonable person actually expects people with disabilities to be cheerful, accepting, and loving all the time. I know I'm not. Neither are the people with disabilities who are my friends. (Maybe, as they will have read that statement by now I should say, 'neither are the people with disabilities who WERE my friends'.)

"YOU CAN'T EXPECT THE WORLD TO CHANGE OVERNIGHT"

This sentence is used by some members of the authorities as a response to a request for a reform. Although it may seem like a bewilderingly inappropriate response to a request, say, for a curb cut at 12th and Main, it's meaning is quite simple. It means "Go away, and put the `DO NOT DISTURB—RIP VAN WINKLE AT WORK' sign back on the door when you leave."

These phrases are all what I call the "curveballs." There are many others, too. Somebody should write <u>A Disabled Person's Dictionary</u> explaining them all someday. Not me, though. I'm too busy trying to be cheerful, accepting, and loving all the time.

Rawnie Dunn

Half-Acc.Ed

"**H**alf a loaf," they say, "is better than none." This means, I suppose, that even if you don't get everything you ask for but do get something, you should be grateful for it because something is always an improvement over nothing. All of which may be true for things like loaves of bread, but just how much better would half of things like an airplane, a cheque, or a pair of pants be? Half of some things, it seems, can still be as useless as nothing at all.

Increasingly, nowadays, you see three symbols for accessibility being used: 1) a wheelchair with a stick figure in it to denote FULL ACCESSIBILITY, 2) this drawing with a line through it to say that the place or event it refers to is TOTALLY INACCESSIBLE, and 3) the same lovable stick-figure in a chair with a wheel made up of dots to indicate PARTIALLY ACCESSIBLE. Personally, I never could figure that last one out. It seems to me that Accessibility is one of those things that either IS or ISN'T, and that being 'Partially Accessible' is a little like being 'Partially Pregnant'.

For example, once I was in a store and suddenly remembered that I had to make an important phone call. I was directed to what the clerk called a "partially accessible" phone booth in the far corner of the parking lot. When I got there I found it had all the requisite features for use by someone in a wheelchair all right, like a widened entrance, eye-level notices, and a lowered phone. It also had an eight-inch curb completely surrounding it. Perhaps it was PARTIALLY ACCESSIBLE to the owners of the store, but after spending a good ten minutes trying to get in, I had to admit that it was TOTALLY INACCESSIBLE to me (which is probably a good thing, actually, because by that time I was using language that shouldn't have gone over the wires anyhow).

Sometimes, Accessibility is an attitude. I've been to many FULLY ACCESSIBLE washrooms where the store personnel had obviously become a little over-excited by the sight of all that empty space in there and felt compelled to stack mops and tin pails and box upon box of cans in every unused inch. Some people may call this Partial Accessibility, but I can't partially use a washroom.

Just what is PARTIAL ACCESSIBILITY supposed to mean, anyhow? Is it when something is only accessible to a person with a disability when she or he is accompanied by an obliging able-bodied person? Is this consistent with the idea of accessibility at all?

Probably the most insidious kind of inaccessibility is the kind that proudly declares itself to be FULLY ACCESSIBLE and does, indeed, have all the right amenities for wheel-chair-users but zip-boom-all for people with other types of disabilities. Recently, I met a deaf student who told a story which illustrates this phenomenon. He was in a study carrel at his school when a loud fire alarm jangled throughout the building. Everybody else cleared out fast but because they didn't have a non-auditory warning system, he didn't even know something was up. Consequently, he was still lost in his books when the firemen came in. They were very angry with him for not leaving like the others did. When he scribbled a quick note to explain that he couldn't do that because the building was inaccessible to him, they said, "What do you mean 'inaccessible'? We have ramps every-where!"

That kind of PARTIAL ACCESSIBILITY—the kind that con-siders the needs resulting from one type of impairment only—amounts to TOTAL INACCESSIBILITY for the vast majority of people with disabilities, including many wheel-chair-users.

Don't get me wrong. I am not totally unappreciative of the effort expended by some people in making a public place Partially Accessible. When people are at least a little aware of the needs of people with disabilities and make even a half-hearted attempt to incorporate features that are accessible to us, I half appreciate it. They will get the other half of my appreciation when they finish the job.

The Integration Waltz

Sometimes you wonder if they think integration is something one "DOES". Particularly if "one" is a man or woman with a disability. I have sat through many pep-talks by cab-drivers, waitresses, government officials, and other would-be social workers, where I, as a disabled person, am energetically told that integration is something that I should be accepting responsibility for myself. You get the odd feeling that they imagine they are in a sweaty locker-room pacing up and down among a group of people with disabilities who are staring forlornly at the helmets they are dangling between their knees; that they think a quietly impassioned speech ending with a rousing, "Now get out there and INTEGRATE!" will send us roaring out of the room and on to win!

They would be the first to acknowledge that the task ahead of "us" is not an easy one. Most of them, I suppose, would be willing to play Sympathetic Bartender and when a battered-looking disabled person arrives, would say with a knowing smile: "Had a rough day integrating, eh?" and as they mixed a double murmur soothingly: "Well, better luck tomorrow."

It's probably appropriate that they take on the bartender-role, since they seem to think an integrated society is something like a cocktail drink—"mix ten-parts of able-bodied organizations with a jigger of disabled individuals. Shake vigorously and voila—INTEGRATION!"

If I only had a nickle for every time I've been told that I must be an "ambassador" for disabled people. "Now remember," someone will say whenever I am about to make a foray, "you must be tolerant but assertive, principled but agreeable, enthusiastic but relaxed, knowledgeable but humble, amusing, candid, and memorable but unobtrusive—and, above all, act naturally." It doesn't really make any difference when I whine: "But I only wanted to use the restroom!" "Integration," I will be reminded, "is the abiding task of every person with a disability."

Well, I have just one word to say to those people when they say things like that. The word is "why?" Why do they get to wash their hands of the whole business and play part-time

Coach/Bartender while we do all the work? Why is integration just "our" duty? Why is it not the duty of everyone, whether they are disabled or not?

It seems to me the problem stems from the commonly-accepted definition of the word "integration". I think that, contrary to apparently popular belief, integration is not an action. It is the name of a social condition. And it will come about only when we ALL accept full responsibility for the society we've created together.